Rites of Passage

A Program for High School African American Males

Shirley R. Butler-Derge

UNIVERSITY PRESS OF AMERICA, ® INC.
Lanham • Boulder • New York • Toronto • Plymouth, UK

Copyright © 2009 by
University Press of America,® Inc.
4501 Forbes Boulevard
Suite 200
Lanham, Maryland 20706
UPA Acquisitions Department (301) 459-3366

Estover Road
Plymouth PL6 7PY
United Kingdom

Library of Congress Control Number: 2008935973
ISBN: 978-0-7618-4320-7 (paperback : alk. paper)
eISBN: 978-0-7618-4321-4

Cover photo by Dr. Shirley R. (Berry) Butler-Derge of grandsons,
Jason M. Towns, 9 and Omari T. Towns, 7.

∞™ The paper used in this publication meets the minimum
requirements of American National Standard for Information
Sciences—Permanence of Paper for Printed Library Materials,
ANSI Z39.48—1984

My son, Shane Mauric
My grandsons, Gabrie

. . . To all the young Afric
remember that there may
however, keep you he
Victory is YC

Contents

MY VEINS
[dedicated to my grandsons]

I have no eyes

Yet I can smell your essence
Its interlocked in my heart
Beats
The dejembe of it all
My child
Your reflections

Ancestors rejoicing at the fishing banks
The day of the coming storm

Your lips round and rosy
Are mine on a snapshot
Of the little feeling the control of it all
Giggling
Poke Out
Poke In
Now blow a bubble

My veins spread the clock to a cedar tree
Yet your taste for love
Blankets me on chilly nights

If the sunshine sits still on me one day
Know peacefully
My veins are your veins
Like the rose to a thick bush

Preface

In this book the writer will examine Rites of Passage programs for high school African American males. Basically the following question will be discussed; (1) Are the Rites of Passage programs for young males a necessary educational tool to improve academic performance and self-confidence? In order to achieve these objectives an investigation of the following components will be discussed, (1) Background of Education for African American Males, (Berry, 1994) (e.g., Description of the Content (Figures 1.0-5.0), Problem Statement (Figures 1–8), Grade Point Averages and Standardized Test (Milwaukee Public Schools, 1990), History and Scope of the Problem (Christensen (1989); Dent (1989); Gibbs (1989); Hare (1989), Hilliard (1986), Major (1990), Kerner (1967); Kunjufu (1989) and Williams (1989), and Problem Significance McClester (1990); Moore (1992). Then, the writer will delve into an effective Rites of Passage model at: Browne Junior School (i.e., (a) Program, (b) Goals/Methods, (c) Modules of Instruction, (d) Retreat, (e) The Initiation ceremony, (f) The Induction Ceremony, (g) Results (Bryant (1991); Chiles (1991). The latter session of this paper will discuss the implementation of a Rites of Passage Program in Rufus King International Baccalaureate High School for African American males. Components in this session are centered around the following subtitles; (a) Identification of the Problem, (b) Definition/Necessitude; Mensah (1999, p. 10)), Gennep (1984, p. 2), (c) Selection Process, (d) Age Group, (e) Objective, (f) Goals, (g) Location, (h) Duration/Hours, (i) Activities and (j) Evaluation (Berry (1994). Given the in-depth research presented in this book, the reader will acquire further information that pertains to the following questions: What is a Rites of Passage program? Are Rites of Passage programs effective educational tools to develop and implement in High School for African American males? And what are some necessary components that must be incorporated when developing and implementing a Rites of Passage program for African American males in high school?

Chapter One

Introduction: Background to Education for African American Males in High School in Milwaukee Public School

DESCRIPTION OF THE CONTEXT

Oftentimes one can understand a problem, its ramification, and solutions possible much more easily if the context in which it is occurring can be explored. This context can be viewed in many different ways. One way is to look at it from a demographic perspective (Berry, p. 4–5).

In the Midwest, as well as many other parts of the county, the Afrikan American population tends to congregate in large cities. This is definitely the case in Wisconsin as approximately 85% of the state's Afrikan American student population is concentrated in the city of Milwaukee and is served by Milwaukee's Public Schools. Another factor that should be considered when analyzing the problem deals with the changing makeup of the Milwaukee Public Schools (MPS) student population. From 1970 to 1982, while Wisconsin's total school age population was decreasing by 21 & the number of Afrikan American students increasing by 3.6%. This fact, coupled with the decrease in the non-Hispanic white population in the city of Milwaukee, has caused a major shift in the ratio of Afrikan American to Euro-American student population. The best illustration of this phenomenon is provided by noting that only one student in four was an Afrikan American in 1970 while more than half to the MPS student body is now make up of Afrikan American (See Figures 1.0 to 5.0) (Berry, 1994, p. 5).

In conclusion, it can be stated that the effort to deal with the problem of low achievement by Afrikan American males must be made within the context of a changing urban school system that has a raising and disproportioned number of Afrikan Americans in relation to the total population of the state as a whole (Berry, 1994, p. 5).

PROBLEM STATEMENT

Leaders of America's business world remind us regularly that applicants come to them ill-prepared to assume even entry level positions in the world of work. Colleges and universities need to explore new admitting procedures and prepare for Afrrikan American applicants. Statistics tell us that this lack of preparation is a greater problem for Afrikan American males than for any other segment of the population (Berry, p. 5).

This comes as no surprise when one considers the direct link between academic and future success whether on the job or in higher education. For it is in school that Afrikan American males demonstrate greater failure than other groups by low rates of achievement on standardized tests and high rates of dropping out of school before graduation (Berry, p. 6).

Significant changes need to be made in the way schools teach Afrikan American males so they become successful in the academic environment. The purpose of this research is to initiate components of that environment to ensure success: high levels of student and teacher expectations, curriculum modifications, parental and community involvement in the educational success, strong and positive role models, a success-oriented support system and finally, meaningful preparation for the work force or for further education (Berry, 1994, p. 12).

The task of verifying the problem of the lack of academic achievement by young Afrikan American males is unfortunately all too easy. The statistical evidence is so overwhelming that after reviewing it, no one should be able to deny that the problem exists (Berry, 1994, p. 12).

The evidence itself will be presented in two parts. The first part will deal with an analysis of grade point average, which was derived from grades as reported on traditional reports cards. The second part will deal with a similar analysis of standardized test scores (Berry, 1994, p. 12).

GRADE POINT AVERAGES

When analyzing grade point averages, it could be argued that grades that appear on report cards are subjective in nature and are not totally indicative of what a student has learned or achieved. If used as a relative measure, they can help provide a part of the picture group or individuals achievement. Unfortunately, the picture painted by this measure is very bleak according to a Milwaukee Public School Task Report. During the 1986–87 school years, Milwaukee's Afrikan American high school students had an average 1.46–point average. Even when one allows for the vagaries of the grading system, it is clear that the level of achievement as represented by the statistic is unacceptable. However, the news gets worse when one analyzes the data of Afrikan American males who maintained a grade point average between 3.0 and 4.0 accounts for only 2% of their total group. Only 17% of the groups were able to maintain an average between 2.0 and 2.9. Any group in which 81% of its members are unable to maintain at least a C average must certainly be judged as having a problem with achievement (See Figure 8.0) Milwaukee Public School, 1990) (Berry, 1994 p. 13).

STANDARDIZED TESTS

Another measure of educational achievement is the standardized test. This type of measurement can also be faulted as not being an accurate method of measuring one's true level of achievement. The additional factor of cultural bias can also be viewed to discount the results. However, as with the use of report card grades, if one uses the results as part of a trend, or if the results show dramatic differences, valid conclusions can be drawn from the data they produce. When comparing the number of Afrikan American students scoring above the national average on norm referenced tests given in 1989 to the number of Euro-American students who score above the national average on norm referenced tests given in 1989 to the number of Euro-Americana students who scored above the average on the same test, one can instantly see a disturbing discrepancy. Even though the percentages vary from year to year and by subject (tests were given in grades 2, 5, 7, and 10 in reading and math). Afrikan Americans in general and Afrikan American males in particular were consistently significantly lower than Euro-American counterparts two to three times the number of Euro-Americans than Afrikan Americans scored at the national averages or better on a percentage basis. Even with the admitted inaccuracies of achievement tests taken into account, it can be stated that as a group Afrikan American males consistently scores significantly lower than their Euro-American counterparts (See Figures 7.0, 7.1 & Table 1) (Milwaukee Public Schools, 1990). Moreover, then we examine the problems cited above in the year 2004 we note that "Increasing poverty and homeless, "are major" . . . barriers in academic achievement for the Milwaukee Public School" district, quoted Superintendent Andrekopoulos (Redovich, 2003). For example, "7,000 to 8,000 MPS students are classified as homeless. More than one thousand MPS youth are incarcerated or in detention for some time each year. Wisconsin's incarceration rate for Blacks is the highest in U.S." Moreover, ". . . in MPS, 90% of high school age students attend 15 large comprehensive high schools with an average enrollment over 1,300 students. Student proficiency and graduation rates in these large comprehensive high schools remain woefully low. The state's 2001–2002 dropout rates fell to 1.935 percent from the prior year's rate of 2,120 percent. Wisconsin had 5,533 of its 286,014 ninth–12th-grade students who left school during the 2001–02 school years" (Redovich, 2003). NICLL concur with State Superintendent Elizabeth Burmaster that, "The presence of even one dropout is troubling," (Ibach, 2003)

HISTORY AND SCOPE OF THE PROBLEM

One cannot address the academic underachievement of Afrikan American males without taking a look at how the problem evolved historically and what, if anything, is presently being done to address the situation. Current research findings demonstrate that, historically, racism has academically [crippled] African American students and has widened the gap between the halves and have-nots. Overwhelming evidence has consistently shown a significant correlation between academic underachievement, low self-esteem and racism (Berry, 1994, p. 19).

Hilliard (1986) and others trace racism to the days of colonial expansion when greed and lust for power created a sick belief system for both the colonizer and those being colonized. Racism, characterized by a distortion of reality, destroyed the victims' identity, thereby claiming superiority of the oppressor. Colonizers accomplished this by destroying the history and culture of their victims and rewrote history to assist their own claim to superiority. Historically, McCarthy (1988) cited that "every academic discipline has been used to justify colonialism and racism. Those in power have controlled, destroyed, distorted and fabricated information." He concludes that, "schools have become sites for producing and making acceptable myths and ideologies that systematically disorganize and neutralize the cultural identifies of minorities.

The result is a U.S. system of education built on Euro-American worldview, which tends to benefit white students, whose cultural patterns and styles are more attuned to this worldview. Students, says Christensen (1989): . . . are subliminally socialized, acculturated and oriented to believe that the Western experience, culture and worldview are superior and dominate.

In a Report of the National Advisory Commission on Civil Disorder (commissioned by President Lyndon B. Johnson after the Detroit and Newark rebellions of 1967), Williams (189) suggests that if you look at the attitudes of Black youth between the ages of 15–24 during the late sixties and compare them to those of Black youth at the present time ". . . there is no significant passed, except in the areas of racial consciousness and identification." Yet in

1967 the typical "rioter" according to Kerner (1967), "felt strongly the he deserved a better job and that he was barred from achieving it not because of a lack of training, ability or ambition, but because of discrimination by employers." There are only one critical difference between Black youth in the sixties and those today, concluded Williams (1989) and that was Black men of the sixties were more solidly grounded in their Black identity and defiantly rejected the racism that eats away at the self-confidence of our young men today.

Kunjufu (1989) further elaborates on the concept of historical racism by describing how Europeans and specifically European-Americans have conspired to destroy Afrikan Americans by changing the lives of Afrikan American boys. He describes in detail how Afrikan American boys are systematically programmed for failure so that when they become adults, they pose little danger to the status quo. He cites the public school as being the most flagrant institution to contribute to this destruction. It is the purpose of this research paper to show what schools can in fact do to counteract this "sly conspiracy."

It is the contention of the writer that schools must do everything in their power to reverse the trend of mounting evidence that suggests that a near majority of working-age Black men ages 15–44 are alcoholics or drug abusers, are in prison, unemployed, infected with AIDS, or suffering from some other life-threatening condition or are slated to die at the hands of other Black men (Williams, 1989). Gibbs (1989) reveals in her landmark volume Young, *Black and Male* in America that "more young Black men died from homicide in one year (1977) than in ten years in the Vietnam War."

Schools, the author contends, need to sound the alarm and call into service whatever it takes to address the plight of young Black males in our cities and in our schools. Gibbs (1987) wrote in Los Angeles Times" . . . young Black males in America's inner cities are endangered and constantly threatened with physical, psychological and social annihilation. They have been misadjusted by the educational system, mishandled by the criminal justice system, mislabeled by the mental health system, and mistreated by the social welfare program."

Some historians (Williams, 1989; Majors, 1990) feel that without a Black struggle to orient them as it has oriented every generation of Black people since 1916, young Afrikan American males will left to their own devices to forge their own identifies in gangs and out of American television and MTV. The result will be a further erosion of racial identity and political clarity, and a continued high suspension rate, high drop-out rate, low academic achievement and low self-esteem. Williams (1989); and Majors' (1990) beliefs are in the city of Milwaukee. Between 1978 and 1985 the Milwaukee Public Schools (MPS) rated third among cities in the nation in suspending more

Black then White students from school. It was also reported during this time that 94% of all students expelled from the MPS were Afrikan American (Milwaukee Public School).

Four questions we concerned citizens must explore at this point are:

1. Why is Afrikan American males being suspend or expelled?
2. Are suspension and/or expulsion an effective way to solve a problem?
3. Who is the problem, the student or the teacher?
4. What impact would the development and implementation of a Rites of Passage program have on the academic performance and self confidence of Afrikan American males in high school?

Dent (1989) shared with the reader a brief senario of a hidden cause-and-effect of most suspensions or expulsions:

> *"Hey, little," the high-pitched voice would yell as Bill entered the gym each day. Bill didn't know what "nigger" meant, but he could tell it was a name-calling, evil word by the mean expression on the white boy's face. One day the boy followed his words with a push, the next day with a punch. Bill told the gym teacher, the white man who told him to play fair, but he shrugged his shoulders. No big thing, his eyes said to Bill. So one day Bill decided to fight back. He "went upside that white boy's head" with his fist, when the boy hit him back, Bill tackled him to the ground. I bet that got the teacher's attention. He grabbed Bill, threw him into the office, pulled out a wooden paddle and laid four hardy strokes across Bill's 6 year old behind. Eleven years later Bill's eyes still flash with anger when he remembers what happened"* (Dent, 1989).

Dent (1989) concluded that when it comes to racism, the public schools are no different from any other American institution, as many educators believe in the negative stereotypes of Black men. These images influence teachers when they teach Black boys and explain why these children fail in school.

Dr. Bruce Hare (1989), an educational psychologist and an associate professor of sociology, at the State University of New York at Sony Brook, stated that teachers and principals are likely to bring stereotypes of Black boys to work with them and a conscious conspiracy to destroy Black males isn't necessary for destruction to occur. Discrimination merely requires that school personnel act according to the existing stereotypes they have; this negative treatment of children tends to become a self-fulfilling prophecy" (Berry, 1994 p. 24).

Supporting Hare (1989), Dent (1989) cites that ". . . the statistics on the academic achievement of Black boys bear this out. According to the U.S. Department of Education, nearly 20 percent of all Afrikan American males drop out of high school, in many cities the percentage is nearly 50 percent. Black boys also score lower than any other group of youngsters on standardized tests. They are disproportionately misclassified and place in classes for the mentally retarded or are locked into slow-learning classes more often and with dire consequences than for any other group of children. And they are suspended, expelled and corporally punished more often and for lesser offenses than White youngsters. They are also less likely to go to college than Black girls, and when they do, they're more likely to drop out."

The harrowing problems that beset Black men later in life—the 5% chance of being murdered, the unemployment rates double those of every other social group, the extraordinarily high chance of being incarcerated—often begin in the classroom (Dent, 1989).

Kunjufu (1986) supports Dent's (1989) report on Black males. He stated, "People don't realize that what happens to boys in school between the ages of 9 and 13 will determine whether they go to college or jail and how much income they will earn in years to come. Every Black male child who is misdiagnosed and placed in special education is a prime candidate to deal drugs."

Gray, program director of the National Coalition of Advocates for Students, national, Boston-based group that studies public-school issues involving poor Black, Hispanic and handicapped students cited, "Things that happen to our kids in school can degrade, dehumanize and socialize them into a condition of inferiority and a sort of passive acceptance of a system they know is wrong. When children are turned off by school, the social institution that was created to enhance their growth and development, they may turn off to society at large, with predictably negative consequences" (Dent, 1989).

Williams (1989), an attorney and educational consultant based in Detroit, completed several studies that supported Dent (1989) Hare (1989) and Kunjufu (1986) reports on Black males. One of Williams (1989) studies on school discipline showed that although Black and White students are tardy for school at practically the same rate, Afrikan American students are disproportionally referred to the principal's office for punishment.

According to Williams (1989), the lack of uniform discipline procedures in most school districts leaves teachers with too much discretionary authority in the administration of discipline, which allows racism to creep into the process. The liberal suspension policies in some school send a dangerous message to Black students.

Williams further stated, "On the other hand, we're telling them about the importance of education. On the other hand, we remove them from school on short term suspensions for minor forms of misbehavior, like tardiness or cutting class."

Sometimes other problems creep into the disciplining of Afrikan American youngsters. "There's the fear factor," adds Gray of the National Coalition of

Advocates for Students. "It's rooted in the history of this country. Black males are the most feared population, which places them under tighter scrutiny in the schools." Gray concluded that this fear leads teachers and administrators to employ more extreme forms of discipline. According to the U.S. Office for Civil Rights, about 5.2 percent of all Afrikan American students received corporal punishment in 1986, compared with 2.8 percent of White students. The National Coalition for Advocates for Students estimates that Afrikan American males twice as likely to receive corporal punishment and to be suspended as there Euro-American counterparts. This high rate of punishment sends a dangerous message to many Black boys: Afrikan American males have no place in the academic world (Dent, 1989).

PROBLEM SIGNIFICANCE

This problem of great significance not only to the population of Afrikan American males but also to society as a whole. Afrikan American males have an unemployment rate that is three to four times that of the national average. Many suffer from a lack of self-respect and self-identity and are unable to support families. This puts a great burden upon society in general and must be dealt with by improving the educational environment, which so far has failed to prepare them for a self-sustaining productive life. (Berry, 1994 p. 25).

State Representative Gwendolynne S. Moore (1992) from Milwaukee, Wisconsin stated, "We must determine the root cause of the problems in our community. The entire country is suffering from the loss of young, vital, energetic lives of Afrikan American boys and men." Ms. Moore concluded that, "It is a tragic, tragic loss of potential. An Afrikan American boy in this country has a 1 in 45 chance of becoming a cocaine abuser, a 1 in 24 chance of being imprisoned in his 20's, 1 in 4 chance of dropping out of school and a 2 in 5 chance of becoming an alcohol abuser."

OBJECTIVES

Overwhelming evidence suggests that unless something radical is done to address the plight of the Afrikan American male, this country will suffer long term losses in terms of the social, political and economic burdens it will have heaped upon an already dismal situation. Prison walls will continue to bulge, business and industry will continue to lament the less-than-adequate preparation of its workers, and taxpayers will continue to reach into already-empty pockets. Social, medical and rehabilitation agencies will continue to place bandages on wounds that are beyond healing.

Schools can no longer ignore the situation the nation, the state and the city are at risk of seriously failing large segments of their population and jeopardizing the lives of many of their citizens. Schools must begin to address the situation and attack the problem with intensity, vigor, and resolve. Schools must begin to focus on what can be done to provide specific and well-defined strategies to address the needs of Afrikan American male students.

Chapter Two

Implementation of Effective School Program Browne Junior High School Rites of Passage

Due to the overwhelming evidence presented in this research paper, the writer strongly believes it is imperative that we focus on an effective junior high school model that has marked a significant impact on the academic performance and self confidence of Afrikan American males. For example, Walter M. Bryant (1991), chairman of Browne Junior High School's Rites of Passage Program in Washington, D. C., cited that, "The Rites of Passage program at Browne Jr. High School was introduced to the student body in the fall of 1989. The program was designed to aid ninth grade students, both male and female, in transition from adolescence to young adulthood. It utilizes the African tradition of manhood and womanhood. It utilizes the African tradition manhood and womanhood training. This training module fit the needs of the students and the community to successfully insure the transition of the student" (Berry, 1994 p. 113).

GOAL(S) METHODS

Additionally, Bryant (1991) stated that, "This program served as a model for the D. C. Public Schools and is beginning to be implemented in other schools in Washington, D. C. The training modules are all instructed after school twice a week with community service activity reserved for Sundays. The length of each session in a module is one hour and thirty minutes. As has been the case in the past, some of our more popular modules may be extended, accordingly" (Berry, 1994 p. 113).

Moreover, Bryant (1991) acknowledged that, ". . . current mentors in our program are all affiliated with the school either as a teacher, attendance officer, or support personnel. Each mentor is responsible for one module of instruction. Outside consultants' resource personnel may be brought into the program as need arises. Currently, we operate with twelve mentors. If there is a mentor who is uncomfortable with a module of instruction to which he/she may be assigned, it is up to that mentor, with the approval of the others, to get outside consultants/resource personnel who have expertise in that area. Each mentor is expected to form, with one or two of the initiates, a Big Brother/Big Sister relationship" (Berry, 1994, p. 113)

Bryant (1991) surmised that, "During the course of the twelve week period of training, the initiates have certain expectations to fulfill." They consist of the following:

1. Uniform Dress—Every Friday
   Boys—Dark trousers, white dress shirt tie encouraged.
   Girls—Dark skirts, White blouse.
3. Eat as a group in school cafeteria with available mentors.
4. Wear the Rites of Passage badge/ribbon daily.
5. Daily check-in with the male or female mentor to whom they have been assigned.
6. During the last week before the induction ceremony each initiate is on is on a *vow of silence,* talking only to their teachers, mentors, administration, and to carry his/her *Rites of Passage Book* in which each of his teachers is to sign off attesting to this vow of silence, performance in class, and other comments which may be justified (Berry, 1994, p. 114).

MODULES OF INSTRUCTION

According to Bryant (1991), the Rites of Passage program consist of twelve modules of instruction. They are:

1. History of Our People—The focus of this module is African history, emphasizing the accomplishments of people of Africa, as well as, the introduction of slavery into this country and the civil right movement in America. *Suggested viewing of "Eyes on the Prize," a PBS documentary on the early civil rights years.*
2. Family History—focus of this module familiarize the student with his/her complete his/her going back as many generations as possible. Each initiate is required to do an extensive family tree. Each initiate is strongly urged to do an oral history on family by taping the various elders of the family, their version/recollection of earliest years, through permanent oral record of their family.

3. Spirituality—[To Be Revised/Inserted Later]
4. Human Sexuality—The focus of this unit is NO "how to" unit. Emphasis is placed on abstinence. However, the same emphasis is placed on prevention of STD and teenage pregnancies. The reality is that many of our students are sexually active demonstrated by the statistics on the rising rate of pregnancies in this country. Additionally, physiological aspects of the human reproductive system are taught Suggested viewing of *"The Miracle of Life," an Emmy award—winning program on the highly acclaimed N series on PBS. If it is available, an episode of "A Different an episode of "A Different World" guest starring Whoppi Goldberg* as a co-professor is an excellent perspective on AIDS. It is on NBC in the spring of 1991.
5. Taking Care of Self—The focus of this module is personal care and proper hygiene as well as nutrient and health. It is in this unit that the *effects of d alcohol and tobacco on the human body* are discussed. It's also in this unit that values consistent with existence this society is reaffirmed. *Rap sessions/open g discussion* are encouraged on values you wish highlight.
6. Housekeeping/Finance—The focus of this module is independent living, responsibility, and realistic financial management. *Emphasis is placed on getting and maintaining a place of residence within their means.* One introduces the concept of setting goals and long range planning. This is further discussed in the Career Development module. The finance component is limited to preparing a budget based upon a hypothetical salary and hypothetical family. The initiate's responsibility is to plan a family budget within strict guidelines of budgeting with strong emphasis on a minimum of 10% savings monthly. *Planning a menu to feed the hypothetical family with a minimum of two balanced meals a day further enhances this process.* After the initial preparation of the menu in 100% of the cases each went well over the allocation for food in the initial budget. At this point each initiate must redo his/her food budget using suggested sale papers and coupons. It may result in changing the initial budget at the expense of some other item it the initiate cannot develop a proper menu under his allocated food budget. Parents often help initiate with this at home or shopping trips. Using the nutrition guidelines developed in the previous module, the initiate should be able to complete their requirement.
7. Career Development—focus of this module is setting goals and long range planning. One introduces the concept that attaining one's goals is a series of stage. In this module the value of education is constantly reinforced as a primary tool of attainment. The work ethnic is also reinforced as a means of attainment. The phrase "Where do you wish to be in 10, 15, and 20 years and how are you going to achieve it?" opens many avenues of possible activities to reinforce the concept of setting goals and long range planning.

8. Time Management/Organization Skills—The focus of this module is the exploration of a means to achieve an end and the concept of time in achieving it.

9. Cultural Arts—The focus of his module is *the appreciation of African art and music* as well as an introduction of the initiates to the African American expression of the arts and music. Also explored is the impact of African music on contemporary music and instrumentation as well as the development of dance. Utilization of community resources such as museums, theater, and concepts to reinforce this module.

10. Community Service—The focus of this module is to emphasis community involvement by actively participating in programs that require the initiate to give of his/her time and energy for the benefit of others. Each initiate is required to give at least *16 hours of service to the activity* which must be documented by either a mentor in the program or an official of the agency in which the service is rendered. All of the activities are done on Saturday except Project Share (A Catholic Charities food distribution program, which is an after school project held every third Friday of the month.).

11. Street Law—The focus of this module is to message is to *encourage and lighten students in all aspects of law enforcement, i.e.,* protections afforded under law enforcement including those provided by local police and federal agencies, and the punitive aspects of law enforcement for offenders. Additionally, police to whom we are all subject will place emphasis on the proper conduct of both parties during routine stops.

12. Values Clarification—The focus of this module is to explore acceptable values consistent with being accepted as adult as well as making decisions that affect the entire process of growth and maturation. Emphasis is also placed on accepting the consequences of ones actions as a result of the decision making process. Since the major focus of the entire program is the development of values which allow full growth of the potential of the initiate, it is suggested that this module be presented to the entire group on the retreat, simply because there is more time to do so.

Upon completion of the twelve modules, Chiles (1991) reported, "The last thing youngsters do before the induction ceremony is go on a three day retreat with their mentor-teachers, usually in Virginia or Maryland. In this setting, the mentors, who each select two little brothers or sisters among the group, are able to spend more time with the youngsters individually to discuss values and goals."

Chiles (1991) concluded that, "The week before the retreat, the youngsters take a vow of silence, which prohibits them from talking to anyone except teachers, administrators and other Rites of Passage members. It's fun to watch people try to break them, and to watch them communicate with others without breaking the vow." Bryant stated that, "This is the beginning of the process that bonds them as brothers and sisters. It also gives them a sense of resolve: I finish this" (Berry, 1994, p. 118).

RETREAT

According to Bryant (1991), when one prepares for the induction ceremony initiates should ". . . be taken on a retreat away form the site of instruction, preferably a two day retreat. It has been our experience to allow the initiates to come up with a budget based on the planning of the menu for the entire stay [module 6], organize the entire schedule for the meals from preparation to clean-up [module 8] develop the PT [physical training] agenda each morning [modules 5 and 8] and to develop some sort of acceptable entertainment for the group during its retreat."

Bryant (1991) also revealed that the "most important component of this retreat is the Naming Ceremony." Each initiate is given an African name based of his/her characteristics as determined by the mentors. The names are selected from *Golden Names for an African People*. It is usually done outdoors at night around a *"Council of Five"* if possible. It is here that the most important part of the retreat takes place. Each initiate explains what the experience has meant for his/her spiritually [module 3].

Bryant also suggested that when one plans for a retreat ". . . try to select a site that is private and isolated to aid in the bonding process that has been developed during the entire instruction periods. Select as many mentors as possible to accompany the initiates on the retreat. *Encourage parental involvement in the process, especially for the naming ceremony.* Campsites are usually the best although college campuses in the spring of the year may be available if the former is not. You may wish to have a theme for the retreat and subsequent induction ceremony. Most importantly plan your retreat to instruct and to have fun" (Berry, 1994 p. 119).

The final two stages for the Rites Of Passage are cited by Bryant (1991) as The Initiation Ceremony, and The Induction Ceremony.

THE INITIATION CEREMONY

According to Bryant (1991), prior to the beginning of the modular instruction, an initiation ceremony is conducted in a school wide ceremony to introduce the initiates. During this ceremony, conducted by an elder or mentor, the initiates receives his/her candle to be lit from a central candle to symbolize the light needed to be guided through this journey in to young adulthood. He/she calls upon an ancestor to guide them through this journey. There is a ritualistic explanation of all symbols used in the ceremony. The symbols used should reflect a value you wish to instill during the instruction process. The Browne's Model used the following five symbols:

1. Portion of Chain Link
2. Woven Basket
3. Large Candle
4. Coconut
5. Large Book of Knowledge
6. Strength/Remembrance/Family
7. Industry
8. Enlightenment
9. The Hardness of Life/Struggle
10. Education/Spiritually

In addition to the above, Bryant added, "Other symbols may be utilized as befits one's program. Finally, all of the initiates pledge in unison the oath that is administered by an elder or a mentor. The initiation ceremony is preceded by a procession of the initiates and followed by a recession. A reception usually follows the culmination of the program" (Berry, 1994 p. 120).

INDUCTION CEREMONY

Bryant stated. "This is a most elaborate celebration of the completion of manhood/womanhood training. All candidates for induction into the Rites of Passage Society are dressed in African clothing. Uniformity is the key here. All males are dressed in the same style carrying a shield of their design. All females are dressed in the same style also. Each candidate is also barefoot. The elders, the mentors, and the previous inductees lead the grand processional. After they have entered, the senior mentor issues the call and response to the elders and the initiates and then the initiates are led into the auditorium, accompanied by ceremony for the inductees, their family members in attendance, the mentors, administration, and guest."

MERIT/DEMERIT SYSTEM

Bryant conducted that; "Each initiate is required to accumulate a minimum of 1500 points during the training period. The points are awarded by the mentors responsible for the ongoing activities of the program, usually a male mentor for the male initiates and a female mentor for the female initiates." Bryant provided the following seven Merit/Demerit points:

1. Wearing of Badges—5 pts. Daily
2. Module Attendance/Completion—20/30 pts.
3. Daily Check-In—10 pts.
4. Friday Lunch/Uniform—25/20 pts.
5. Maintenance of Journals—100 pts. Max or 80% of 100
6. Community Service—25 pionts/hour
7. Performance Sheet—25 pts./week

RESULTS

"We find that kids very often don't respect one another. These boys and girls learn to work together and learn respect," says Walter Bryant (1991), a biology teacher at Hugh M. Browne Junior High School and chairman of the Rites of Passage program here. "We started to try to implement the values that are missing. There are some exceptional children here who want to learn and have nobody to teach them these things. And there's peer pressure—a lot of then don't get out of this environment long enough to get anything else" (Berry, 1994, p. 121).

Chiles (1991) added "Making it through to the induction ceremony isn't easy—the privilege is earned. The students meet the 12 mentors—teachers after school two days a week. First they get a firm grounding in African and African American history to help them understand where they come from. As part of these lessons, they are required to construct a family tree. The first time, some students realize that there are successful, professional people in their families. Next they learn about finance and budgeting. They are give imaginary families and an imaginary income for which they have to plan a budget (Berry, 1994, p. 122).

"It's quite astounding for them to see you don't start a job making $65,00," Bryant says. "You can't go out and buy a Porsche right away. So how do you get it? By getting an education" (Berry, 1994 p. 122).

Bryant instructs the 25 students in sex education and AIDS education. He commented that, "Most of these kids still think it's transmitted by homosexuality, when in fact a great many of these cases in D.C. are from IV drug use" (Berry, 1994, p. 122).

According to Chiles (1991), ". . . community service is the most important part of the training students receive. The youngsters are taught to give back to their community—even if they get nothing in return. They make Easter baskets to bring to homeless shelters; they volunteer once a month at a home for orphaned or abandoned children and even conduct an Easter -egg hunt there. They also volunteer at a nearby senior citizens home. In return, some of the senior citizens participate as elders in the induction ceremony in accordance with certain African traditions, which say that elders must give their permission for the youngsters to pass into adulthood (Berry, 1994).

"The community service teaches them they have responsibility to their community. They see that their situation may be bad, but there are always others whose are worse," says Carol O'Brien, a school attendance officer and mentor in the program (Chiles, 1992).

Chapter Three

Implementation: Rufus King International Baccalaureate High School

IDENTIFICATION OF THE PROBLEM

During October 2002, at Rufus King International Baccalaureate High School in Southeastern Milwaukee, Wisconsin's database report showed a student population at 1399. Of the total of high school students, 54% are African American (males 244; girls 535), 4.8 are listed as Asian, 3.3% were Hispanic, and 35% were Caucasian. 60% of the African Americans stated during a interview that they were frequently suspended for the following, wearing hats and/or jackets, listening to music with their headphones, chewing gum, tardiness, lack of supplies, profanity and/or walking in the hall without a pass, fighting, skipping class, and walking out of class without permission. They also added that if they walked in the hall with a white student without a pass, they would be stopped and questioned, not the white male. Moreover, recent data showed that out of population of 244 African American males 145 students' grade point averages was at a 2.00 or below. These reactions strongly support Berry (1994), Dent (1989), Hare (1989), Kunjufu (1986) and Williams' (1989) research on school discipline.

Additionally, 40% of the junior and senior African American male students made statements such as: "We need more African American teachers and we don't understand why we have white teachers teaching us African American classes." One student gave an example of a hallway encounter with a white teacher who was on duty. "When I pass the teacher in the hall to enter my classroom, he shouted at me to take my cap off my head. I told him that it was not a cap, it was my African hat. It is called a Fofe'. Nevertheless, he shouted back, "I don't care what you called that thing on your head, I said to take it off or I will call security to escort you to the office." I males cited previously, the writer decided to develop and implement a pilot Rites of Passage program to record its presence to note if it would make a positive influence on students' academic performance and self-confidence. However, prior to designing Rites of Passage for the students cited in this book, the writer decided that it is imperative that we examine what are the Rites of Passage.

DEFINITION

Mensah (1999), stated that from Joseph L. Henderson, M. D.'s in-depth study on rites of passage, data revealed that, ". . . from ancient times to the present, initiation, as a body of knowledge, has often been forgotten and then discovered. It traces the development of initiation early in the 20th century, with the publication of *Le Rites de Passage* by Arnold Van Gennep in 1906." Gennep ((1906) written works shown that, ". . . initiation of boys was considered as a mere record of brutal devises invented, supposedly to frighten boys into becoming men" (p. 3).

Additionally, Mensah (1999) acknowledged that Gennep (1906) viewed ". . . these so called brutal devises as educational processes for accelerating growth. He saw that the various rites in each process of initiation made possible a passage from one stage of existence to the next stage." Gennep (1906) summarized that, ". . . initiation is not only for a man's right for admission to a Man's House, but that women also need to be made women by means of appropriate rites—beginning with early menstrual rites and culminating in the marriage ritual" (p. 3).

Moreover, Mensah (1999) observed from Dr. Henderson's previous in-depth study on initiations that there is a relationship between ancient times and ". . . modern initiatory experiences that show how certain essential transitions in psychological developments are made." He surmised, ". . . the sense of such rites—as in the so called puberty rites–always has been expressed as the need to outgrow, regressive childhood patterns and to become adapted to the social group" (p. 7).

Concurring with Dr. Henderson's belief, Mensah (1999) defined the Rites Of Passage (NRP), ". . . as a developmental process through which individuals in a group experience breakthroughs in their psyche and are enabled to discover and act upon who they are and what they were born with, but have been lying dormant, until their breakthroughs. A breakthrough into his definition is a major psychic achievement that enables further spiritual development in a person" (p. 10).

was so shocked and hurt. I was also suspended for 3 days until my fath
came to school."

Another freshman African American male stated, "I don't understand h
we happened to get a white teacher teaching us about African /African Lit
ature. It's like we don't have educated Black people who can teach us ab
ourselves. They don't know what its like to be Black. It could make m
sense to have someone from your own culture teach you about yourself." /
ditionally, a senior added, "I know I would learn and appreciate learn
about myself from someone who knows and understands what I have exp
enced." Overall, these experience call to mind Kunjufu's (1989) observati
on the appropriateness of using teachers with a limited Eurocentic persp
tive, which may harm the education of youngsters. Overall, the African An
ican males felt that most of their white teachers didn't respect them and t
didn't want them in the building.

Due to the overwhelming evidence presented in this paper, that Afri
American males are not achieving academically and that their self-co
dence is being destroyed, the writer firmly believes that it is imperative
we focus on developing and implementing a Pilot *Rites of Passage l
grams* for African American high school males in order to ensure acade
achievement and positive images for African American males in School
in the communities. Supporting this belief, Mahdi (1997) stated that, '
our present day Western civilization is an exception in the history of
because of its lack of rites of passage for the young adolescent Th
some formal rites still do exist such as Confirmation, Bar Mitzvah, gra
tion and driver's license) most young people are left to make or disc
their own challenges or rites of initiation on." Moreover, in the past s
that there may be many factors that may have led to African Ame
males not succeeding in public schools, nevertheless, the question sti
mains ". . . what, if any can the public school system do to help in the
sition from childhood to young adulthood so that some of these prol
might be reduced?" (p. 24).

RITES OF PASSAGE PROGRAM

The results of Mahdi's (1997) current research on the rites of passag
grams for youth revealed that, "The psychological effects of the rites s
to result in the internalization of a positive self-concept for each initia
competent and capable young adult, ready for new responsibilities." Il
tion, "The rites helped the young adolescent become a responsible cal
the culture" (p. 26). Therefore, given the experiences the African An

MISSION STATEMENT

The title of this Pilot Rites of Passage program for African American high school students is OKRA (The original spirit of God). Its Mission statement is "Strengthening the Community by Focusing on Issues that Impact African American Males."

ELIGIBLE

Students who are eligible for the Rites of Passage Program must be:

- African American Males (Females may be included)
- In Grades 8–12
- Maintaining a grade point average of 1.00—3.00 or better
- Needs improvement: Attendance and Suspensions
- College bound
- Good Character

SELECTION PROCESS

Based upon the criteria described above, 35 *(numbers may vary)* African American 8th and 9th grade junior and high school students will be randomly selected by parent, staff and community members to participate in the *Okra*'s Rites of Passage program.

STUDENT/PARENT CONTRACT

Students are required to sign a contract to state their commitment to the Rites of Passage program. Parents/Guardians' also sign to state their commitment to assist the student while they are engaged in the rites of passage program (Note sample contract):

I [STUDENT'S NAME] agree to participant in the rites of passage program for African American Males for four months. As a participant, I promise to be commitment toward enhancing my inner gifts in the following areas (leadership, academic, self, creative expressions, culture and community), to continuously uplift nature and mankind.

I [PARENT'S NAME], parent/guardian agree to support my child [STU-DENT'S NAME] while he/she is participating in the Rites of Passage Program.

GOALS/OBJECTIVE(S)

Okra's Rites of Passage has identified the following project goals which will be targeted through its program activities:

1. To increase skills among students to resist peer pressure through leadership development and training;
2. To increase the knowledge of students of negative consequences of involvement with negative behaviors such as substance abuse, violence and high risk sexual activity;
3. To increase awareness of cultural values and their natural heritage;
4. To improve academic performance and increase awareness of careers and educational opportunities;
5. To provide on-going support for program participants through mentoring by African American males; and
6. To increase parent and community involvement by 90% by one year.
7. To provide educational enrichment, support and guidance to students who have promise but are not yet demonstrating their full academic potential.
8. Students will increase their writing skills with percent accuracy.
9. Students learn to utilize effective communication skills.

LOCATION

Educational, recreational and cultural innovative activities are implemented and conducted at school and related sites throughout different neighborhoods and communities in Milwaukee, Wisconsin. Each site or center will operate one class hour during/ (students may earn credits), after school three days a week for 45 minutes and on weekends (once a month on Saturday for 2 hours). Each session will provide a safe atmosphere for youth to participate in a range of activities. These activities will include life skills and leadership development training, tutorial program programs, cultural awareness and education programs, field trips, sports as well as arts and crafts activities.

DURATION/EVALUATION

The duration of *Okra's* Rites of Passage program for high school African American males will consist of 5 months (August through January). Participants will meet once class period, once a day. All participants will receive credit and will receive homework assignments. Participants are also required to attend one weekend session for training/tutoring for 2 hours. Students and parents will a written contract acknowledging their commitment to the program. The effectiveness of the program will be measured by the following components, (a) Students with a low or above academic performance must continue to show gain or remain on the honor roll; (b) Each student must exhibit leadership ability; (c) Each student must demonstrate self-confidence and a knowledge of his heritage; (d) Each student must improve his attendance by 90 per cent; (e) Suspension rate must be reduced by 90% per cent; (f) Each student must demonstrate an ability to effectively communicate with their peers, parents, and staff members. Every six weeks, two methods will be used to measure each student's progress. These two methods will consist of bi-weekly self and peer evaluation, and a six weeks parents and teacher survey and/or interview evaluation.

ACTIVITIES

Okra's Rites of Passage program for junior and high school African American males will evolve around educational achievement, community responsibility, leadership development, pride, cultural awareness, and social. Specifically, at the beginning of each activity a ten-minute libation exercise will be conducted by an appointment elder to invite the ancestors to shield and guide the youth toward a productive day. Moreover, the following daily activities (*note duration/evaluation for time length for more detail*) are scheduled around the student to ensure academic achievement, cultural awareness and a positive image of self:

History of Our People

1. The focus of this module is African history, emphasizing the accomplishments of people of Africa, as well as, the introduction of slavery into this country and the civil right movement in America. *Suggested viewing of "Eyes on the Prize," a PBS documentary on the early civil rights years* (Berry, 1994, p. 114).
2. Family History: focus of this module familiarize the student with his/her complete his/her going back as many generations as possible. Each initiate is required to do an extensive family tree. Each initiate is strongly urged to do an oral history on family by taping the various elders of the family, their version/recollection of earliest years, through permanent oral record of their family (Berry, 1994, p. 114).

3. Spirituality: This exercise is called "We Like That! Students will use a container to make an Mzuir (means good in Kiswahili) box for their classroom. This box is to be used to recognize their peers when they do positive things that they appreciate. For example, if Travis shares his calculator with you, write on a small piece of paper, Travis shared his calculator with me (Kunjufu, 1993, p. 15).

4. Awareness: According to Mahdi (1997), "The purpose of this unit was to help the students become aware of the concepts of transition: rites of passage, death-rebirth and psychological transformation. The goal was to give them cultural perspective and a frame of reference to help them understand that the changes they are going through (or about to make) was universal and a normal part of life. The procedure for this exercise consist of the following steps: (1) first introduce the students to the words: "anthrop lists and rites of passage, shown slide of Australian aboriginal puberty rites (National Geographic Magazines 1980), and read excerpts from Nkwala "Transition Stories," end chapter). The unit closed with a discussion of the theme of life as a journey (Mahdi, 1997, ps. 26–27).

5. Understanding: The objective of this unit is to "facilitate a deeper understanding of the process of change for each of the students. The unit focused on memories from childhood, signs that indicated they were growing up, and past, present and future fears. Part of this understanding of change concentrated on their life-line by helping them see where they have come from, where they are now, and what they hope to achieve in the future" (Mahdi, 1997, p. 27).

6. Challenges: This unit was designed with simple challenges to provide students with positive strategies to handle "certain developmental task." Therefore, "This unit starts with the students developing their own modern rites of passage and ends with a "Declaration of Dependence. . . . One of its goals was to increase the communication flow between young adolescent and parent, realizing that this can be a very difficult task for some adolescents and for some parents." After each exercise student is are allowed to orally read their written comments and discuss it with their class (Orally reading this activity may be optional) (Mahdi, 1997. p. 27).

7. Male/Female Responsibility: The purpose of this event is to give African American males an opportunity to discuss male issues with other males/females. The event will be a workshop on Male/Female Responsibility. Young African American males will learn and share male experiences. African American males will discuss the following, (i.e., love, fatherhood/motherhood, education, community involvement, sex, and spirituality, etc.) *(Data will be collected during and after the event, both observation and written student reports will be utilized)* (Berry, 1994, p. 87).

8. Classroom Corporation: Students will form their own classroom corporation. They will then decide upon a product or a service that be appropriate to market to other student/parents and faculty member. They will also advertise, take orders; collect money, record, report, produce, and deliver. At the end of this activity, they will be able to keep their profits. At the completion of this program, African American males will be able to demonstrate an improved knowledge of the world of work and how business functions. (Invite Black business entrepreneur as guest speakers and/or mentors) (Berry, 1994, p. 97).

9. Creative Writing/ Storytelling: Participants will attend a six week creative writing workshop titled, AARUSI (AH ROO SEE) (a Swahili word which means a "wedding." Students will creatively learn to write and share their experiences in life poems, short stories, rapping, or plays. In addition, storytelling participants, parents, grandparents will share creative stories of their past as well as their present (Berry, 1994, p. 141).

Follow-Up Reading: Orally Read by the Instructors

Blach, F. (1959). *Brave Riders*. New York: Thomas Crowell. With an accurate portrayal of Indian culture, this book describes a young boy's initiatory journey into manhood. Ages 10–13.

Bates, B. (1978). *The Ups and Downs of Jorie Jenkins*. New York: Holiday House. Through parental illness, a young adolescent girl begins to make important decisions for herself and becomes aware of her importance to the family. Ages 10–14.

Craig, J. (1969). *No Word for Good-Bye*. Toronto: Peter Martin Associates young teenager after efforts to save the aboriginal land of an Ojibwa group in Manitoba fail. The entire band disappears and the young protagonist realizes that in the Ojibwa language, there is no word for good-bye. Ages 12–15.

Distad, A. (1977). *The Dream Runner*. New York: Harper & Row, 1977. A contemporary story of a young boy who sets off on his own vision quest and finds "something to live up to." Ages: 10–13.

Frank, A. (1952). *Ann Frank: The Diary of a Young Girl*. New York: Doubleday. The maturation of a young girl over a two-year period. Describes her relationship to her changing body, her parents and her first love. Ages: 11–14.

Haig-Brown, R. (1962). *The Whale People*. London: Collins. A young man of the Hotsath tribe, Atlin, receives both practical and spiritual guidance to prepare him to take his father's place as the whale chief. The daily activities of life on the West Coast of Vancouver Island before magnificent whaling scenes highlight the English settlers came. Ages: 12–14.

Jones, W. (1968). *Edge of Two Worlds*. New York: Dial Press. Set in 1842 this beautiful story describes a mentor relationship between a fifteen year-old white boy and an Indian silversmith –teacher. Ages: 10–14.

L'Engle, M. (1980). *A Wrinkle in Time*. New York: Dell. A young adolescent girl, struggling with feelings of hopelessness, plays a key role in helping her family. Ages: 10–14.

McKenzie, J. (1971). *Rivers of Stars*. Toronto: McClelland & Stewart. Fifteen-year-old Andy, a West Coast Indian boy, takes his injured father's place on a fishing boat for the summer. He meets with hostility from some crewmembers and is aided in coping with prejudice with the help of an elderly fisherman. Ages: 12–15.

Major, K. (1978). *Hold Fast*. Toronto: Clarke, Irwin. Michael's parents are killed in an automobile accident and he is sent from his Newfoundland out port home to live in the city. Local bullies at the new school attempt to terrorize him and Michael's opposition to their threats creates moments of conflict and suspense. (A sensitive exploration of early adolescence by an author who was a teenager when it was written.) Ages: 12–16.Mildiner, L. 1981. Getting the eagle. London: Macmillan. A contemporary story set in the East End of London, describing a failed vision quest. Ages 12–16.

O'Dell, S. 1981. *Sing Down the Moon*. New York: dell. Spanish slavers capture a fourteen-year-old Navaho girl. She escapes only to be evicted from her homeland. A poignant tale of Navaho life, including rites of passage. Ages: 10–14.

Shaura, M. 1976. *Seasons of Silence*. New York: Atheneum. A young adolescent girl comes to terms with family problems, painful feeling death, loss of friendship, and the beauty and healing powers of nature, life and love. Ages: 12–16.

Sperry, A. 1940 *Cal it Courage*. Toronto: Macmillan. The solo journey by boat, of a fifteen-year-old South Sea Island boy who survives terrible storm and wins his manhood. Ages: 10–14.

Sutcliff, R. 1982. *Warrior Scarlet*. London: Puffin Books. After three years in the boy's home, Drem must kill his own wolf to prove the right to wear the warrior's scarlet. But how can he do this when his right arm is useless? Ages: 10–13.

Wojciechowsak, M. 1964. *Shadow of a Bull*. New York: Athenaeum. Usi the metaphor of bullfighting, the psychological struggle of a boy, separating his identity from that of a famous father is describe. Ages: 10–14.

Daily Journal Writing

Students will write daily their thoughts for 20 minutes at the end of each class. At the beginning of each session students will orally read their journals to the class (Note sample journal below):

Part A: Sample Journal

1. My African American name is:
2. My African name is:
3. Today's date is:
4. Write the day of the week you were born:
5. My age is:
6. My parent(s)/Guardian was born:
7. I was born:

Part B: Writing Guide

1. Write what you saw today that excited you.
2. Write what you did today that was enjoyable.
3. What did you share with someone today?
4. What did you notice today that you never observed before?
5. What do you see yourself doing 20 years from now?
6. What are you doing to prepare yourself for your future?
7. State what is unique about you.
8. Draw a picture of yourself (Use color pencils or markers).
9. State two things you have accomplished that make you feel proud.
10. State two people in your family you appreciate. Briefly state why.

Cultural Awareness

Students must know and honor the following:

1. "The Black National Anthem"
2. The Seven Principles of Kwanzaa
    (a) Umoja = Unity
    (b) Kujichagulia = Self-Determination
    (c) Ujima = Collective-Work & Responsibility
    (d) Ujamma = Cooperative Economics
    (e) Nia = Purpose
    (f) Kuumba = Creativity
    (g) Imani = Faith
3. Select one African American and learn everything you can about that person's life. In short, you become a "walking book of his/her life. Take this knowledge and share it with the community (i.e. African Festival, libraries, Black history programs etc. . .).

National Black College Tour

Students will attend a National Black College (e.g., note suggested list below) tour with their elders. While on campus students will attend workshops that focus on: admission, financial aid, dorm life, class scheduling, books/fees, tuition and staff support (Berry, 1994, p. 58).

Suggested List

Tennessee State—Nashville, Tennessee 37203
Meharry Medical College—Nashville, Tennessee 37028
Fisk University—Nashville, Tennessee 37203
Alabama State—Montgomery, Alabama 36195
Tuskegee University—Tuskegee, Alabama 36088
More house College—Atlanta, Georgia 30314
Spelman College—Atlanta, Georgia 30314
Clarke Atlanta University—Atlanta, Georgia
Morris Brown—Atlanta, Georgia 30314
Hampton University—Hampton, Virginia 23668
Virginia State University—Petersburg, Virginia 23803
Virginia Union University—Richard, Virginia 23220
Howard University—Washington D. C. 20059
Dillard University—New Orleans, Louisiana 70122
Gramling State University—Gramling, Louisiana 71245
Jackson State University—Jackson, Mississippi 39217

Peer Tutoring/Mentors

This activity is called "Kunji". Kunji is a Swahili word, which means to pass one's craft to another. "All people are born to succeed. No one is born to be left behind" (Mensah, 1999). Three days a week, after school, African American males will receive supervised academic support from their peers (i.e., pairing low achievers with high achievers.

METHOD USED TO MEASURE PROGRESS: PRE/POST TEST & STAFF SURVEY: (BERRY, 1994, P. 70)

Sample Questions

A—Excellent, B—Satisfactory, C—Needs Improvement
Directions: Circle your response and return to the facilitator

1. Academic Achievement—A B C
2. Behavior—A B C
3. Completed Assignments—A B C
4. Participation—A B C

STUDY SKILLS

Students will increase their study skills by 90% within one year through participation in a course specifically designed to meet their academic learning styles. For example, when a student has demonstrated that it may be difficult for him to understand a new concept by listening to a lecture, a teacher/team will work with this student to give the same concept but by using a hands-on experience/visual/musical/ and/or computer approach on—understand a new concept.

Within this team, a study skills group will be formed to address the needs of low achieving African American males. The study group will focus implementing new learning approaches to increase the students' ability to prepare for testing, ask questions in class, and organization skills. Students will meet with staff members after school for one hour for the entire school year. Students will retain in the study group until they have demonstrated academic success.

Summer Enrichment School

Students are required to participant in a 6 week summer session from 8:00AM to 12:00 noon. Summer session are designed to strengthen leadership, academic skills, career skills, self, cultural pride and male/female responsibility. Thus, classrooms and assignments are centered on community quest speakers (e.g., NTU International Rites of Passage Institute, 100 Black Men association, and other working professionals), field trips and seminars. Addition, school counselors (high/college) are provided for students to assist them with selecting and preparing for their career choice. Weekly awards are also given to students who perform exceptionally well on weekly quizzes, genuine effort, and for excellent attendance.

Evaluation: Pre & Post Survey

Directions: Briefly write a response to the following two questions:

1. State a negative experience you encountered last year in school/community.
2. Briefly some strategies you used to turn your negative experience into a positive event.

UNIFORM DRESS

Every Friday African American males/females will wear dark trousers, Black shirt with a Kente cloth scarf (African attire is encouraged). Students are assigned the same lunch hour to allow them to sit together for 4 months (snacks are permitted only on Monday & Wednesday). In addition, "during the last week before the induction ceremony each initiate is on a vow of silence, talking only to their teachers, mentors, administration, and to carry their Rites of Passage Book in which each of his teachers are to sign off attesting to this *vow of silence,* performance in class, and other comments which may be justified (Berry, 1994, p. 114).

Mother/Father (Significant Female & Male) and Daughter/Son Banquet

The objective of this event is to increase parent involvement by 70% each month and to allow African American students an opportunity to experience leadership, organization, decision-making, communication planning, budgeting and to work with other male members of their families on a cultural project. Students with their Mother/father and significant other African American adults will discuss and plan a dinner banquet once a month. The mothers/fathers select a Guest speaker with their daughters/sons. Location, time, volunteer parents and students will arrange equipment. Mothers/Fathers and daughters/sons prepare a soul food dinner. This event will reflect a black, red and green color theme. Moreover, informal interviews will be conducted at the end of this event to measure what the students learned about leadership, organization, decision-making, communication planning, and budgeting *(Awards and verbal announcement of student's accomplishments are made at the end of the banquet)* (Berry, 1994, p. 80–81).

RETREAT/CAMPING/FISHING

This event was developed to provide an opportunity for African American females/males, mentors and their families and opportunity to spend 3 days out of the city to learn about nature, themselves and others. Prior to attending this event, student, mentors, parents and staff members will plan a daily schedule for activities, cleaning duties, and a food menu. Gathering wood, building a campfire, fishing, and care of their living quarters (tent), is added responsibilities students will experience.

MERIT/DEMERIT SYSTEM

Students initiate are required to accumulate a minimum of 610 points while participating in the Rites of Passage program. The points are awarded by the mentors (e.g., staff, parents,), responsible for the ongoing activities of the program. Mentors are African American females/males.

Merit/Demerit Points

1. Wearing of Kente cloth/African Attire—90 pts. Fridays/Cultural Knowledge
2. Academic/Attendance/Behavior—95 pts.
3. Peer Tutoring/Leadership—100 pts.
4. Lunch/Diet—75 pts.
5. Maintenance of Journals—75 pts.
6. Community Service/Workshops—75 pts.
7. Performance Sheet—100 pts./week

Chapter Four

Naming Ceremony

Each initiate is given an African name based of his characteristics as determined by the mentors. The names are selected from *Mensah's (1999), textbook.* This event usually occurs outdoors around a fire. However, it may be performed in a building if the weather is not appropriate. Each student explains what the experience has meant for his personal growth. Students are encouraged to invite 10 relatives/friends to come and share this experience with them. You may wish to have a theme for all three ceremonies (Berry, 1994, p. 119).

THE INITIATION CEREMONY

Preceding the curriculum-designed activities for the Rites of Passage program, an initiation ceremony is perform in a school wide auditorium to introduce the initiates. This ceremony is performed by an elder and/or mentor. Each student receives a candle to be lit in the center to represent the light that guides him through his journey into young adulthood. He appeals to his ancestors to guide them through his journey. "There is a ritualistic explanation of all symbols used in the ceremony. The symbols used should reflect a value you wish to instill during the instruction process." *Okra's* rites of Passage program will use the following ten symbols:

1. Kente Cloth Scarf
2. Woven Basket
3. Large Candle
4. Sweet Potato
5. Large Book of Knowledge (the journal)

6. Strength/Remembrance/Family
7. Industry
8. Enlightenment
9. The Hardness of Life/Struggle (one small bottle of water & one small bottle of lemon juice)
10. Education/Spiritually

Additionally, "Other symbols may be utilized as befits one's program. Finally, all of the initiates pledge in unison the oath that is administered by an elder or a mentor. The initiation ceremony is preceded by a procession of the initiates. A reception usually follows the culmination of the program" (i.e., a breakfast/luncheon with family, staff, mentors and community members) (Berry, 1994, p. 120).

INDUCTION CEREMONY

"This is a most elaborate celebration of the completion of manhood training. All candidates inducted into the Rites of Passage Society are dressed in African clothing. Uniformity is the key here. All males are dressed in the same style carrying a shield of their design. Each candidate is also barefoot. The elders, the mentors, and the previous inductees lead the grand processional. After they have entered, the senior mentor issues the call and response to the elders and the initiates and then the initiates are led into the auditorium, accompanied by ceremony for the inductees, their family members in attendance, the mentors, administration, and guest" (Berry, 1994, p. 120).

EVALUATION/CONCLUSION

As a group, African American high school females/males exhibited behaviors that have tended to restrict their ability to lead productive satisfying lives. Several authorities including Asa Hilliard (1986) and Cameron McCarthy (1988) point to the early days of the colonies as the beginning of this problem. A racism that destroyed the African American males' self identity coupled with an educational system based on the Euro-American view successfully destroyed any chance that African American males could, in any meaningful way, complete with their white counterparts and participate fully in society. Jawanza Kunjufu (1986) has stated that there is an actual conspiracy to systematically program African American boys for failure so that there is no chance for them to upset the status quo of white domination. The above-mentioned authorities as well as others feel that a specific effort must be made to undo this situation or such things as street gangs and made to undo this situation or such things, as street gangs and MTV will be the dominant forces that forge the African American male identity. This would result in a further erosion of racial identity and declining achievement by this group. Finally, if this large group of African American males is not sufficiently educated for the future, who will care for the middle aged people today? Who will become the fixed income aged population of the future? (Berry, 1994 p. 99).

At the time, African American males are at the bottom of the educational strata authorities such as Dent (1989) have noted that rates of dropouts, suspensions, and failures of 20 to 50 percent have been for this group. They have been seriously disciplined much more often than their counterparts. There has been a disproportionate number assigned to remedial or slow learner classes. African American men have a 5% chance to being murdered and a much higher chance of being incarcerated. These factors as well as countless others have all worked together to send African American males the message that they don't have a meaningful part to play in school or society in general (Berry, 1994 p. 100).

Significant changes need to make in the way schools teach African Americans. The purpose of this program, *Okra's Rites of Passage*, is to initiate components of that environment to ensure success: student, and teach expectations, innovative curriculum, parental involvement in the educational success, strong and positive community mentors/elders, a success-oriented support system and finally, meaningful preparation for the work force or for future education. Therefore, the rites of passage program is designed to specifically address and improve the academic achievement and self-confidence of American females/males in high school. Activities centered on the rites of passage for African American school-aged men will be implemented over a three-month period. While engaged in this program all participants should use the following four basic questions to evaluate the activities' progress:

1. Do the activities mentioned have a positive effect upon the African American females/males in the group?
2. Is it possible for the school to overcome all negative environmental effects that has cumulatively caused a lack of success within the group?
3. What is a reasonable outcome that should be expected?
4. If the program is successful, will it be possible to replicate it with other groups in other locations which are similar circumstances? To answer these questions a two-tired approach of evaluation should be utilized.

Quite obviously the first form of evaluation should deal with the bottom line, which is academic achievement. The African American male's grade point averages and standard test scores should show improvement if the *Okra's Rites of Passage* program has been successful. A simple comparison of the scores that were attained before *Okra's Rites of Passage* program was enacted with those attained after the group has completed the program should shed considerable light on its effectiveness. However, the data would be incomplete without additional evaluation of the individual components of the program. This is necessary for two reasons. The first, it is not reasonable to assume that all of the components have successful or unsuccessful just because the program in total is judged to be one or the other. It is very possible that a successful program might have several parts that may need improvement or were not appropriate when compared to the overall goal of the program. The converse is also true in the sense that program deemed to not have met its goal might still have some positive outcomes in certain selected areas. The second reason for individual activity evaluation deals with the issue of replication. In order to make a decision in this area, it would be important to understand precisely what it was within the group that made it successful in the locality that it was tried. Because local conditions differ, the ability to successfully transplant a program from one to another should not be assumed *(Note other evaluation methods: Appendix II—Staff & Appendix V—Student)* (Berry, 1994, p. 101).

Additionally, there are two limitations to *Oka's* Rites of Passage program for junior/high African American females/males, and they both deal with environment. The first limitation is that many young African American females/males are forced to deal with issues that are not necessarily school related. There are many larger societal pressures such as gangs, poverty, and dysfunctional families, which the project's activities may not fully deal with, and which will quite likely have an impact on how well they react to the program. The second environmental limitation on *Okra's Rites Of Passage* for junior/high African American males relates to the type of situation the African American male will find himself in once his school days have been successfully completed. Institutional racism, lack of funds for college, and lack of job/business opportunities are but a few of the obstacles to be faced even if all of the other problems such as lack of self confidence and self-identity have been overcome. However, it can be effectively argued that African American females/males with healthy self-concepts and good skills stand a much better chance of living positive, productive lives than those who feel they have no hope (Berry, 1994, pp. 101–102).

CONCLUSION

In short, we will all suffer if we don't see that it is time to review and explore new methods to teach and reach African American high school students. We can't continue to teach one way and expect all African American students to color Columbus's ships and later recite the constitution without questioning its purpose.

The problems, which confront African American males, are enormous. For example, Coates (2002) stated that, "violence is the number one problem affecting African American males in this country and represents a serious social/school as well as health problems. Because of the negative behaviors or the inability to resolve conflicts in a non-confrontational manner, the leading cause of death among African American males ages 15–24 is homicide. A disproportionate number of African American males, approximately 25% are imprisoned or are on probation. African American males when compared to other populations in the United States resent the highest rates of high school dropout, unemployment and underemployment. While the life expectancy for all other segments of the population continues to increase, the lifespan of African Americans male is decreasing. HIVAIDS, substance abuse and homeless have all had a heavy impact the African American male. . . . Considering all of the problems which confront African American males, there are limited social supports available to African American males" (Coates, 2002 p. 3).

Today African American children, especially males, are screaming for help. They need our love, commitment, guideless, our success stories, our heroes, the elders, and positive professional role models/mentors to long up their sleeves and design a program that will address their needs. A program that wills them the support they need to transcend from one stage of life into another. Thus, the implementation of a Rites of Passage program for junior /high school African American students is the instructional tool that will provide a meaningful goal to successfully in school. Consequently, all African American students will experiences a sense of purpose, direction, and wholeness. With their new growth, the African American adolescent is able to contribute to the making of whole communities, which nourish and supports succeeding generations instead of the dysfunctional urban mental and physical destruction too many of us have witnessed today (Berry, 1994, p. 125).

Appendix One

Group Helps Black Students Learn Self-Respect

by Tannette Johnson

It's not as simple as ABC.

Education must include the basic skills reading, writing, and arithmetic. But to succeed, it also has to set imagination free. it sometimes has to pierce layers of distress and despair from the world outside the school walls. Belief in the potential of children and hope for their future is its bedrock.

Throughout the Milwaukee area, teachers are teaching more than ABCs. Some of them received grants this year from the Greater Milwaukee Education Trust to help run projects they developed for their students. The series will look at six of those projects.

When Shirley Berry began teaching at Riverside University High School last September, she didn't like saw of the things she saw.

"It seemed like African American boys were lost," said Berry, who teaches students with learning disabilities."

"I noticed the same black boys were either in the hall, late for class or sitting in the principal's office for disciplinary problems. I started listening to these boys and felt there's got to be someplace these kids can turn to for help."

Berry decided she would help by starting an African American male support group.

The group is called Umoja, a Swahili word the essentially means "to survive for and maintain unity in the family, community, nation and race, Berry said.

Umoja's goal is to help black male students build positive self-images, perform well academically and learn more African American culture.

"The only way these kids are going to get a sense of pride is for them to know their own history," Berry said. "It bothers me that I didn't see any posters or exhibits at the school accenting black. I saw Spanish culture high-lighted, but nothing of blacks."

Berry who is black, doesn't believe that only black teachers can reach black children. Rather, she said, all teachers should be educated to deal with culturally diverse students. "We have to make teachers more aware of different cultures and help them develop effective methods to deal with those cultures."

Umoja promotes activities and projects that highlight the achievements of blacks.

As an example to students, berry dresses in African clothing and wears her hair in cornrows, a traditional African hairstyle. "I saw a lot of students wearing the African symbol, but they didn't know what it means." Berry said.

"I wore American clothes, but now I wear an African outfit every day. I felt that if I'm going to teach African culture, I should look the part."

Berry, an author with an 18–year old son, received a $1,000 grant from the Greater Milwaukee Education Trust this year. The grants are given to help innovative programs developed by teachers.

The grant will be used mainly to but educational materials and supplies and to help pay for field trips and seminars for Umoja, Berry said.

Umoja began on an experimental basis in October, and 200 students have participated so far, Berry said.

Daudi Shabaka, 17, a riverside senior, says he feels better about himself since he joined the support group.

"The program teaches young black males respect for ourselves and others around us, said Shabaka, who plans to architecture.

"We discuss our problems and try to solve them as a group. We talk about our past and our ancestors. Knowing where you came from really changes the way you think of yourself."

Although the program is aimed at male students with poor attendance records, low grades and frequent discipline problems, many who belong to the support group are succeeding in school.

These students serve as role models and peer leaders for students who have been failing, Berry said.

Berry said she is disturbed that many young black mans do not think positively about their experiences.

"I have each young man tell me something positive that happened to him each week, just t encourage positive thing. It can be that they went to their favorite movie, " Berry said.

"It was difficult for the boys at first. Some of them would say that nothing good happened to them."

One of Berry's success stories is a 17-year-old Riverside senior who earned good grades but was quiet and withdrawn and showed little interest in having friends or participating in school activities.

Berry helped to bring the youth out of his shell by casting him in the lead role in a school play about the late Rev. Martin Luther King Jr.

"When I first saw him, I felt this kid has something special," Berry said. "I saw so many leadership skills in this young man, so I chose him to be in the play. When he got up on stage, he became Martin Luther King Jr."

"Everyone at school has begun to recognize him for his leadership qualities. Now when he walks down the hall, he floats."

For Berry, seeing the excitement in the her students' faces when they master something new is a rewarding experience.

"I really get excited when I introduce something new to the students and they begin to take it in little by little," Berry said. "You see them going through the learning process, step by step, and gaining knowledge. I enjoy seeing children learn. I love to watch them grow."

Although many teachers stick to the school setting for educating children, Berry uses the community as her classroom. "Since I've been teaching, I've never really stayed in the classroom" Berry said. "I like to walk around the community. When we're not in school, my kids will see me in their neighborhood.

"Sometimes I see them sitting on their front steps, and I'll sit down with them and talk to them. They're really surprised that you stop to say hello to them."

Beverly Lawrence, a teacher aide at Riverside who liked Berry's Ujoma idea and decided to lend her support, serves as the group's co-facilitator.

"I heard about it and felt it would be a good way to give our young men a sense of pride and purpose," Lawrence said. "This program doesn't solve all the problems, but at least it attempts to address some of them."

The project was not received well by some teachers and staff members at Riverside, Berry said.

"I received some opposition from staff members, whom felt, because I'm a female, I shouldn't be running a program for males. Some teachers went to the principal, calling me a racist because I was meeting with African American boys."

Statistics show that many black males are not succeeding in Milwaukee Public School or nationally.

The erosion of the family structure in the black community has contributed greatly to the structure in the black community has contributed greatly to the failure of black male students," Berry said. When you look out your door and see people lost to alcohol, and drugs and your parents are struggling, it affects how well you do in school."

Berry, who has taught in Milwaukee Public Schools for nine years, believes all children can achieve.

"Teachers must become more resourceful in teaching our children, Berry said. "I view the school as a community. We have to do more in the classroom to make their learning experience better."

—from The Milwaukee Sentinel
August 27, 1990

MPS Milwaukee Public Schools Department of Staff Development

PROFSSIONAL GROWTH EVALUATION

Please respond to the statements below by circling a number code.

Strongly Disagree—1
Disagree—2
Agree—3
Strongly Agree—4

1. This workshop was relevant to my current position/responsibilities. (1—2—3—4)
2. The workshop had clearly identifiable goal and objectives. (1—2—3—4)
3. The arrangements (preliminary information, scheduling and physical Facilities) were satisfactory. (1—2—3—4)
4. The instructor was knowledgeable about the topic. (1—2—3—4)
5. I acquired knowledge/information and skills that are beneficial. (1—2—3—4)
6. I have a positive professional attitude toward the topic presented. (1—2—3—4)
7. This workshop fostered greater professional collegiality. (1—2—3—4)
8. I would recommend this workshop to a colleague. (1—2—3—4)

ADDITIONAL COMMENTS

Future staff development I need is:
[Please return this evaluation to the instructor or planning committee]

Student Cultural Afrikan American Survey

Name:
Date:
Event/Activity:

Instructions:

1. Write two things you learned during this activity.
2. Write one thing you learned about Afrikan American culture you did not know before this activity.
3. What did you like most about this activity?
4. If you were to plan this activity for other students, what would you Keep/Change? and explain why.
   I would keep:
   I would change:
5. Describe any feelings you may have had (and wish to share) about your Afrikan American heritage during this activity.

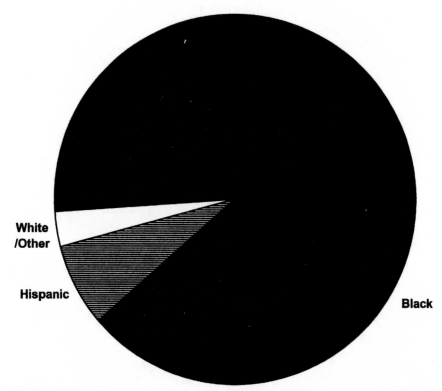

Figure 1.0.   Instilling the thirst for Knowledge: How to Increase the Academic Performance for Afrikan American Males by Dr. Shirley R. (Berry) Butler-Derge Aku Nzingha
Ekua (1994) (6).

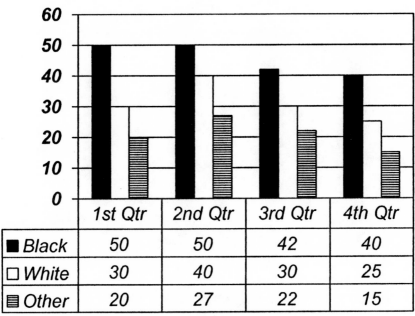

	1st Qtr	2nd Qtr	3rd Qtr	4th Qtr
■ Black	50	50	42	40
□ White	30	40	30	25
▤ Other	20	27	22	15

Figure 2.0.   THE TASK FORCE. Illustrates that the vast majority of Wisconsin's African American students are educated in the Milwaukee Public Schools.

Instilling the Thirst for Knowledge: How to Increase the Academic Performance of Afrikan American Males by Dr. Shirley R. (Berry) Butler-Derge [AKU NZINGHA EKUA} (1994) p.5.

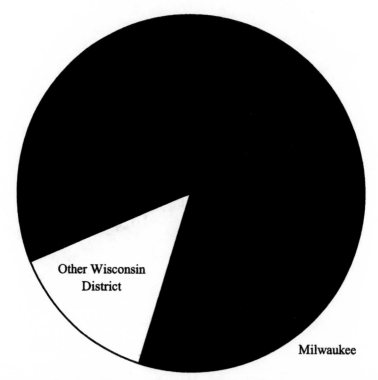

Figure 3.0.   Milwaukee, like most other large urban areas, has experienced a decreased in the number of non-Hispanic whites living in the city (Milwaukee Urban League Report, 1988). As indicated in Figure 3.0. 27% of Milwaukee's residents are minority.

Instilling the Thirst for Knowledge: How to Increase the Academic Performance of Afrikan American Males By Dr. Shirley R. (Berry) Butler-Derge Aku Nzingha Ekua (1994) (8).

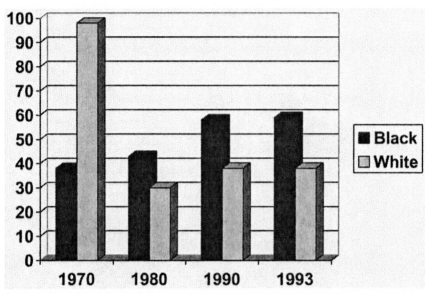

Figure 4.0. The Task Force. The past and projected enrollment data for Milwaukee Public Schools (MPS) depicted in Figure 4.0 suggests the system has slowly changed from a predominately white student population in 1970 to a system with more than half of the students identified as African American.

Instilling the Thirst for Knowledge: How to Increase the Academic Performance of Afrikan American Males by Dr. Shirley R. (Berry) Butler-Derge Aku Nzingha Ekua (1994) (9).

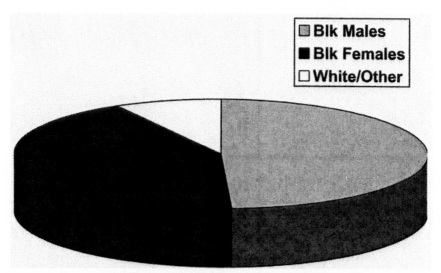

Figure 5.0. In 1970, one in four students in the Milwaukee Public Schools are minority, today more than half of the students are minority. As indicated in figure 5.0, 57.7% of the students currently enrolled in Milwaukee Public Schools (MPS) are American.

Instilling the Thirst for knowledge: How to Increase the Academic Performance of Afrikan American Males by Dr. Shirley R. (Berry) Butler-Derge Aku Nzingha Euka (1994) (10).

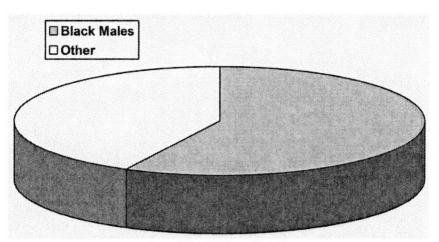

Figure 6.0.   THE TASK FORCE. Slightly more than one-fourth of the 93,000 students currently enrolled in the Milwaukee Public Schools are African American male students. However, as indicated in figure 6.0, approximately one-half of the suspensions are Black males. Additional data (See Appendices) suggests that Afrikan American males, more than any other identifiable group, are least likely to finish high school and are more likely to be suspended or expelled.

Instilling the Thirst for Knowledge: How to Increase the Academic Performance for Afrikan American Males by Dr. Shirley R. (Berry) Butler-Derge Aku Nzingha Ekua (1994) (11).

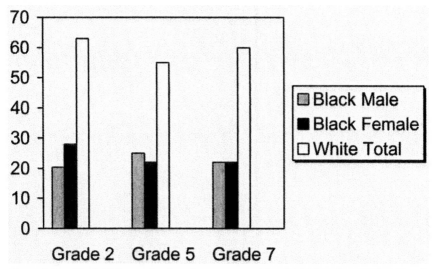

Figure 7.0.   The initial examination data generated by the Milwaukee Public Schools indicates that Afrikan American males are disproportionally underachieving in both reading and mathematics (Figure 7.0 and 7.1).

Instilling the Thirst for Knowledge: How to Increase the Academic Performance of Afrikan American Males by Dr. Shirley R. (Berry) Butler-Derge Aku Nzingha Ekua (1994) (16).

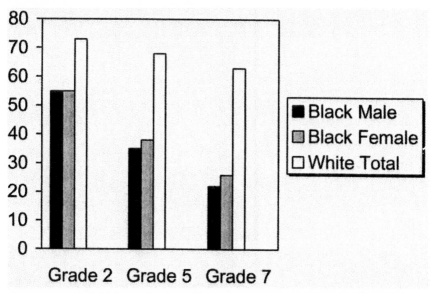

Figure 7.1.   The initial examination of data generated by the Milwaukee Public Schools indicates that African American males are disproportionately underachieving in both reading and mathematics (Figure 7.0 and 7.1).

Instilling the Thirst for Knowledge: How to Increase the Academic Performance of Afrikan American Males by Dr. Shirley R. (Berry) Butler-Derge Aku Nzingha Ekua (1994) (17).

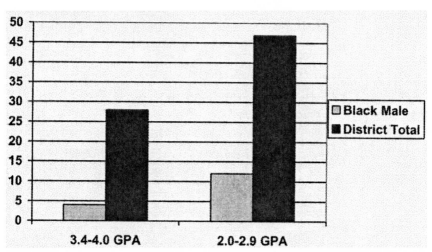

Figure 8.0.   Grade Point Averages. ". . . The number of Afrikan American males who maintained a grade point average between 3.0—and 4.0 accounts for only 2% of the total group. The 17% of the group were able to maintain an average 2.0 and 2.9. Any group in which 81% of its members are unable to maintain at least a C average must certainly be judged as having a problem with achievement (See Figure 8.0) (Milwaukee Public Schools) (Berry, 1994).

Instilling the Thirst for Knowledge: How to Increase the Academic Performance of Afrikan American Males by Dr. Shirley R. (Berry) Butler-Derge Aku Nzingha Euka (1994) (12–13).

Table 1. **Standardized Test Results for Grade 10, Fall 1987–1988**

Instilling the Thrist for Knowledge: How to Increase the Academic Performance of Afrikan American Males

by Dr. Shirley R. (Berry) Butler-Derge Aku Nzingha Euka (1994) (18)

DISAGGREGATED BY RACE/HIGH SCHOOL

School	Total Enrollment	Percent African American	Reading Black	White	Math Black	White
Bay View	1851	40.9	19	52	22	52
Cluster	1308	61.9	17	38	21	38
Hamilton	1826	43.4	19	66	15	63
Juneau	910	56.2	20	49	12	57
King	1191	52.9	68	92	58	95
Madison	1821	59.5	18	61	18	64
Marshall	1320	64.1	17	66	14	60
Mil.H.S./Arts	736	39.7	34	72	27	71
Milw. Tech	1907	38	45	80	58	77
North Division	1256	98.2	13	NA	14	NA
Pulaski	1884	34.2	9	38	6	42
Riverside	1648	48.4	43	81	43	72
South Division	2045	24.4	13	35	12	40
Vincent	1723	54	15	55	15	58
Washington	1608	64.3	25	55	17	47

Bibliography

Berry, Shirley R. *Instilling the Thirst for Knowledge: How to Increase the Academic Performance of Afrikan American Males.* Milwaukee, Wisconsin: Blackberry Creations/ Nzingha's African American Children Publishing Company, 1994.

Bryant, Walter. *Rites of Passage: The Browne model. Browne Junior High School.* 26th St. & Benning Rd., N. E. Washington, D.C. 20002, (202) 724-4547, 1991.

Coates, D. & Evans, P. *Phi Beta Sigma Fraternity, Inc.* NU Sigma Youth Services. Nu Sigma Chapter Web Page, 2002, 3.

Chiles, Nike (1991). "ABC's Project Primer. Interface Institute" *Essence Magazine* May 5, 1991, 9–12.

Christensen, C. P. "Cross Cultural Awareness Development: A Conception Model" *Counselor Education and Supervision.* June 3, 1989, 270–289.

Dent, D. J. "Reading, Rating and Rage: How Schools are Destroying Black Boys " *Essence Magazine*, November 20, 1989, 45–48. Gibbs, J. T. "The Future of Black Men". *Essence Magazine*, November 1, 1990, 1989, 50–52.

Gennep, A. V. *The Rites of Passage.* The University of Chicago Press, Chicago, 1906.

Hare, B. *Readin, Ritin and Rage: How Schools are Destroying Black Boys. Essence Magazine*, November 10, 1989, 49.

Hilliard III, Asa. G. *Free Your Mind: Return to the Source—African Origins.* Atlanta Georgia State University, College of Education, 1986, 10–12.

Ibach, M. "Dropouts Decline, Graduation Rate Increases in 2001–02 SPR: Burmaster: Four Year's Old Data Show Hopeful Trends in Meeting New Wisconsin Promise". *Education Reform* Feb. 28–March 7, 2003. Volume 6, Number 23. Ed. State of Wisconsin: Department of Public Instruction, 2003.

Kerner, A. "The future of Black Men" *Essence Magazine* November 5, 1990, 53–55.

Kunjufu, Jawanza Dr. *Countering the Conspiracy to Destroy Black Boys* VOL.II, Chicago, Illinois: African American Images. SETCLAE self-esteem through culture leads to academic excellence (1993 First Ed., Second Printing) Chicago, Illinois: African America Images, 1986.

Mahdi, L.C. *Betwixt and Between: The Initiation of Youth. Transition from Childhood to Adolescence: Developmental Curriculum*. LaSalle, IL: John Allan and Pat Dyck. Open Court 23–26; 38–39, 1997.

McCarty, C. "Rethinking Liberal and Radical Perspectives on Racial Inequality in Schools" *Harvard Educational Review*, August 1, 1988.

Mensah, Anthony. J. African Centered Adult's Rites of Passage Initiating Adults through the roots of an African (Akan) culture, Milwaukee, Wisconsin, 1999.

Moore, Gwendolynne S. "Black Males" *Milwaukee Courier Newspaper*. March 1, 1992, Vol. XXIX, 11–16.

Milwaukee Public Schools. "Educating African American Males: A Dream Deferred"*African American Task Force*. May 4, 1990, 6–13.

NCCPBE. *Northern California Council of Black Professional Engineers*. 8500 Street, Oakland, CA 94621: Interface Institute, 1991.

Redovich, D. 181 Poverty and Accountability in the Milwaukee Public Schools. Center for Study of Jobs & Education in Wisconsin and United States.November 5, 2002, Education Writers Association. EducationNews.org. 2003, 1–5.

Williams, Strickland. "The Future of Black Men." *Essence Magazine*. November 17, 1989, 52–53.

Index